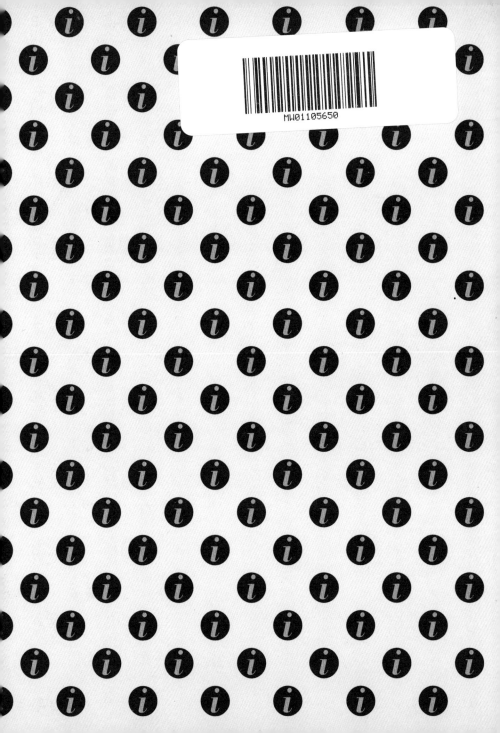

WRISTWATCHES

The new compact study guide and identifier

WRISTWATCHES

The new compact study guide and identifier

Isabella de Lisle Selby

CHARTWELL
BOOKS, INC.

A QUINTET BOOK

Published by Chartwell Books
A Division of Book Sales, Inc.
114 Northfield Avenue
Edison, New Jersey 08837

This edition produced for sales in the U.S.A., its
territories and dependencies only.

ISBN 0-7858-0776-4

This book was designed and produced by
Quintet Publishing Limited
6 Blundell Street
London N7 9BH

Creative Director: Richard Dewing
Designer: Ian Hunt
Project Editor: Kathy Steer
Editor: Jane Donovan
Photographer: Paul Forrester
Picture Researcher: Isabella Selby

Typeset in Great Britain by Central Southern
Typesetters, Eastbourne
Manufactured in Singapore by Bright Arts Pte. Ltd.
Printed in China by Leefung-Asco Printers Ltd.

The material in this publication previously appeared in
Wristwatches by Isabella de Lisle Selby

ACKNOWLEDGMENTS
Special thanks to Richard Leyens and Tina Baldwin.
Thanks also to the Antique Watch Co., London for
providing wristwatches for photography and to the
following manufacturers for supplying photographs:
Audemars Piguet · Baume et Mercier · Blancpain ·
Brietling · Cartier, London and Paris · Dunhill · Girard
Perregaux · Gucci · Hamilton · International Watch
Company · Jaeger-LeCoultre · Jean Lassale · Longines ·
Movado · Omega · Piaget · Rado · Raymond Weil ·
Rolex · Rotary · Swatch · Tag-Heuer · Tissot · Vacheron
et Constantin · Zenith

CONTENTS

INTRODUCTION

MAN'S FASCINATION with passing time has been apparent for centuries, and over the years watchmaking has been revered as evidence of the natural dexterity of human beings. Long before production lines came into being, a cottage industry existed in Switzerland, France and Germany where poor farmers, after trying to make a living from infertile soil during the summer, would spend long winters producing, cog by cog, the forerunners of today's wristwatches.

Although the first portable timepiece was supposed to have been worn by Marie Antoinette in the eighteenth century, the first true wristwatch was not invented for another century. Patek Phillipe is thought to have made the first wristwatch in 1868, but some say that Alberto Santos-Dumont, who was conducting experiments with an "airship," mentioned to his friend, watchmaker Louis-François Cartier, how inconvenient it was to pull out his pocket watch whilst at the controls of his flying machine; when Santos-Dumont completed his record-breaking 240-yd flight in 1907, he was wearing the first Cartier Santos-Dumont.

The aim of this book is not to tell you what to collect, but rather to help you decide for yourself by showing you the variety of watches available. The focus of your collection might be the date of production, materials used or the functions of the watch; or you could base

it on a theme, such as military watches. The following pages will help you decide which way you want your collection to grow and help you in your search for that elusive piece. Some watches have their place in history, others are linked to great sporting events. This book will help you through the collecting maze and point out some of the pitfalls, but, whatever the motivation for your collection, you should start with pieces that please and arouse your interest – a purchase based on price or rarity alone may be regretted.

Big towns, little towns, even small villages have jewelry shops which sell both old and new wristwatches. Do not hesitate to ask if they have anything else apart from the goods displayed, for treasures have been dug out of boxes lying at the back of dusty stockrooms.

Another way to see a variety of pieces and to buy the more collectible item is to visit your local auction room. Articles to be sold can be viewed before the sale and auction house catalogs can be a valuable source of information. Auctions have well-trained staff who are happy to help.

In order to buy intelligently and to keep your collection growing, you need information and facts – after all, to collect is to be constantly learning. There are watch collections in one form or another in most major towns, where both public museums and private collections are good sources of information.

ABOVE EARLY TWENTIETH CENTURY PRODUCTION LINE HIGH UP IN THE SWISS MOUNTAINS. THE WOMEN WERE ALL VERY YOUNG AND WERE CLOSELY SUPERVISED BY THE PATERNAL FIGURE IN THE BACKGROUND.

Many watch manufacturers have their own private collections which may be visited by appointment. The Longines headquarters at St Imier in Switzerland, for example, has its own private museum which houses some pieces of historical importance. Visiting both private and public collections will help you to decide which way you want your collection to go, and which theme or topic you wish to follow. There is a list of useful addresses on page 77.

A wristwatch collection has one advantage over most others in that you can wear your collection on a daily basis, swapping your watch in accordance with your mood, dress or occasion. By reading, observing and visiting museums, stores and sales you will gradually expand your knowledge.

WHAT MAKES
A WRISTWATCH TICK?

O N THE MARKET today there are three basic watch movements: hand-wound, automatic, and quartz. Hand-winding and automatic are referred to as mechanical. It is important to know which is which, as a hand-wound watch will not start when shaken but most good automatics will start when wound.

THE MECHANICALS

The hand-wound wristwatch is the direct descendant of the key-wound pocket watch which acquired a winder, or a crown and stem.

The automatic movement has a long history: it was first recorded in 1770, and in 1780 the pedometer movement was first mentioned. It was an Englishman, John Harwood, who was responsible for the first automatic wristwatch. He originally began experimenting in London in 1917 and applied for a Swiss patent in 1923. The wristwatch that he

perfected was unusual even by today's standards: as it could be set only by turning the bezel (the metal surround frame holding the watch glass) and had to be shaken to be wound. Prior to this all wristwatches were hand-wound.

THE ELECTRO-MECHANICALS

The advent of miniature batteries designed for hearing aids in the 1950s inspired a French company, LIP and an American manufacturer, Hamilton, to join forces for research purposes, and, as a result, the first electric wristwatches were made available in 1957. These models were quite large, ugly and not popular – with one notable exception, the Accutron. Created by a Swiss electronics engineer and with an accuracy of 99.9977 percent, it was issued with the first guarantee of accuracy for a wrist-watch by its manu-facturer, Bulova.

THIS AMAZING WATCH WINDS ITSELF!

N EW as the hour and sound as Big Ben. The very latest in watches—the Harwood. Wearing winds it. Dust and damp cannot enter. The movement is of the best. Ask to see it at any high-class Jeweler's.

Ladies and Gents Wristlets in 9ct. Gold for 8 Guineas.

HARWOOD
SELF-WINDING
WRIST WATCH

Guaranteed and fully serviced by
The Harwood Self-Winding Watch Co. Ltd., Dept. WI, 252-260, Regent Street, London, W.1

THE IDEAL ✕ WATCH ACHIEVED !

ABOVE A 1929 ADVERTISEMENT FOR A REMARKABLE BRITISH INVENTION — A WATCH WOUND BY WRIST MOVEMENT ALONE.

ABOVE ZENITH AUTOMATIC MOVEMENT. THE PLATE BEARING THE MANUFACTURER'S NAME IS THE ROTOR WHICH PROVIDES THE POWER TO THE MAINSPRING.

THE FIRST QUARTZ WRISTWATCH

Quartz clocks had been in existence for some time before quartz watches. In the 1960s, thanks to miniaturization, electronics engineers in Japan and Switzerland were working towards the first quartz wristwatch. Finally, in 1968, both countries had prototypes. These, when submitted to rigorous laboratory testing, proved to have a small margin of error: only two seconds per day. It now seemed to the manufacturers that the rational method of telling the time with a dial and hands should be superseded by something more in keeping with the watch's revolutionary movement. Liquid crystal displays (LCDs) and light-emitting diodes (LEDs) were used. It became apparent that these methods had a number of disadvantages linked to the display. This, plus the fact that these watches could be produced very cheaply in the Far East, soon moved the LCD and the LED production out of the traditional watch-making areas.

The Swiss watch houses went back to the dial-and-hand display which, coupled with quartz technology, can account for some of the most outstanding-looking timepieces of today.

All watch movements work on the same principle. The **time divider** which divides passing time into equal parts must receive power from a **power source**. This power must be transmitted from the latter to the former, so there must be a system for **power transmission**. Finally the watch must show the time after the time divider has completed its task. The time can be shown either on a dial or on a digital display.

OTHER WRISTWATCH COMPONENTS

CRYSTAL

One of three materials is used for the crystal or glass dial cover: plexiglass, crystal and synthetic sapphire. The third material has the same molecular structure as natural sapphire but has been produced in a laboratory. It is expensive and used on higher-quality pieces or watches made for rough sports usage. Older sports watches tend to come with a plexiglass crystal, since until recently, it was only possible to shape the sapphire glass into a level surface, unsuitable for some sports watches. Quartz crystal, somewhere between plexiglass and sapphire crystal in strength, is used on "everyday" watches.

MATERIALS

Disregarding any precious stones which may be present on a watch case or bracelet, the list of materials used by the watchmaking industry, both past and present, is as extensive as it is varied. Gold has been used since the beginning. Most versatile of metals, it is used in both heavy sports watches and equally well in tiny elegant cocktail pieces.

WHAT LOOKS LIKE GOLD . . .

Rolled gold was used widely prior to the 1960s, before technology made gold plating a better proposition. It is not always easy to differentiate between the two materials, though most gold plate has a slightly "harder" shine when given a polished finish.

Silver has also been employed in the manufacture of wristwatches, but not nearly so extensively as stainless steel. The latter metal is the material that is most commonly used for sports watches, with or without the addition of gold or gold plating. Stainless steel is virtually unalterable and it is possible to find quite early wristwatches made of steel which show few signs of wear and tear.

Other materials used in the more contemporary pieces include several organic materials: rock, shell and wood. Man-made materials include ceramics, tungsten carbide, strontium titanite, fiberglass and plastic.

STRAPS AND BRACELETS

When a wristwatch is made, either a strap or bracelet is incorporated into the design, the choice depending on the intended use of the watch. Although earlier pieces usually had leather straps, with extensions for wearing over

WATCH MOVEMENTS

	MECHANICAL	QUARTZ
Time division	Balance wheel	Quartz crystal
Power source	Mainspring	Battery
Transmission of power	Gear train and escapement	Integrated circuit
Showing the time	Motion work (dial train)	1 In the case of the analog watch, the stepping motor moves the hands on the dial 2 For digital watches, the impulses control the liquid crystals or the light-emitting diodes

ABOVE FRONT AND BACK VIEW OF A VACHERON
CONSTANTIN MECHANICAL CHRONOGRAPH. THE LITTLE
NEEDLE AT THE TWELVE O'CLOCK POSITION ON THE
BACK IS THE REGULATOR AND PERMITS FINE
ADJUSTMENTS TO THE TIMEKEEPING.

sportswear, metal bracelets soon followed because they were more durable or stylish.

If the metal bracelet is the original, it will be of the same material as the watch case. It will probably be stamped with the manufacturer's name or logo. If a leather strap is used, check the buckle: if it is the original, it will have some identifying marks on it.

It is very important to look over the strap or bracelet when buying a vintage wristwatch, mainly for safety reasons (see page 71). If the strap or bracelet has deteriorated beyond repair or is absent,

try to replace it with one as close as possible to the original design. In some cases the manufacturer may be able to assist you with information as to what the original strap or bracelet design was like.

WATER RESISTANCE

Both the case back and the crystal need to be held firmly in position to maintain the water resistancy of the watch. From 1927 onwards, watches have been manufactured that are water resistant. Since then, greater efforts have been made to produce watch cases that are more and more watertight and able to withstand much higher levels of water pressure.

ANTIMAGNETISM

Apart from moisture, magnetism is the other main problem for a watch movement. We are surrounded in our daily environment by electrical equipment which gives off a powerful magnetic field and this can adversely affect the moving parts of a watch. Magnetism will affect any watch parts which are made from ferromagnetic substances: for example, iron, nickel or cobalt. The parts concerned with the accuracy of the watch are generally the most vulnerable.

The International Watch Company (IWC), of Schaffhausen, has done much research into antimagnetism. Their flagship piece in this range is the Super-antimagnetic Ingenieur, which is able to withstand a strong magnetic field and is worth having in any collection.

INTERESTING & COMPLICATED MOVEMENTS

THE PRIMARY FUNCTION of watches is to tell the time. They do, however, do a lot of other things which can be used as criteria for a collection. Be it quartz or automatic, a complicated movement can only add to the intrinsic value of a watch, as well as having visual appeal.

The collector's main concern is the beauty of the wristwatch itself, and the hours of labor that have gone into creating it. Such watches need not be prohibitively expensive, for with care and research it is possible to find some very interesting pieces at reasonable prices. This section is designed to help you recognize what you are looking at when you encounter it.

When you have bought a watch with a complicated movement, handle the mechanism with care, especially when no instructions are available; do not attempt to adjust it or set the various displays until you are sure that you know what you are doing. If necessary, find an expert. In fact, although the watch may look complicated, this is rarely the case and once you have mastered the basic technique, you will find that there are few variations.

THE WORLD TIMERS

With the increase in travel for both business and pleasure, it has become more important to have a watch on which the different time zones can be seen. The principle of the time zone movement is simple: a rotating disc is marked with the name of a major city from each of the twenty-four time zones and an extra set of hands or another dial will track the time of the chosen zone. For a long time there have been watches that are capable of giving the time in two different time zones and even keeping track of two different dates.

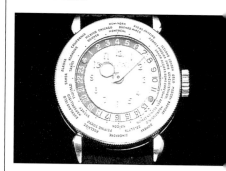

ABOVE A WORLD TIMER BY PATEK PHILIPPE.

POWER RESERVE

The *réserve de marche,* or power reserve, is a feature found on some automatic wristwatches, sometimes paired with another feature such as a world timer, but quite frequently by itself. The power reserve indicates how many hours the watch will run, if left untouched.

MINUTE REPEATERS

A minute repeat movement is the only one which tells the time by sound and it appeared in wristwatches at the beginning of the twentieth century. At the push of a button, the watch can be set to strike the hours, quarter-hours and minutes. The idea behind this type of movement is simple: before luminous paint, it was not possible to tell the time in the dark visually, so another method had to be found – hence the minute repeater. A pioneering company is Audemars Piguet, which claims to have produced the smallest minute repeater movement in the world. Audemars Piguet is also unusual in that it produces a rectangular minute repeater, which certainly adds to the collectibility value.

ABOVE EARLY MEMOVOX BY JAEGER-LECOULTRE, 1950. THIS ONE IS MADE FROM PINK GOLD AND HAS AN AUTOMATIC ALARM MECHANISM.

ALARM WRISTWATCHES

One of today's most famous alarm wristwatches is surely the Grand Reveil by Jaeger-LeCoultre. A most interesting feature is the alloy used for its gong, which dates back to the Chinese Bronze Age when it was well known for producing a clear and pure sound. This gong is kept separate from the movement so that its vibrations will not have a detrimental effect. Another of Jaeger-LeCoultre's famous products was the

THE GREAT MAKERS

Audemars Piguet · Baume & Mercier · Blancpain · Breguet · Breitling · Cartier · Chopard · Corum · Dunhill · Ebel · Georg Jensen · Gérald Genta · Girard-Perregaux · Ingersoll · International Watch Company · Jaeger-LeCoultre · Longines · Movado · Omega · Patek Philippe · Piaget · Raymond Weil · Rolex · Rotary · Tissot · Ulysse Nardin · Vacheron Constantin

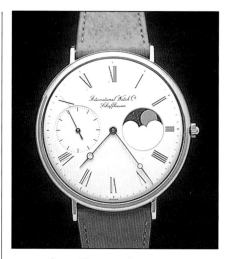

ABOVE POCKET WATCH ON A STRAP: UNUSUAL
MOONPHASE BY INTERNATIONAL WATCH COMPANY.
THE SECOND HAND IS AT NINE O'CLOCK AND THE
MOONPHASE INDICATOR AT THREE O'CLOCK.

Memovox wristwatch, made during the
1950s, which was the first automatic
wristwatch to have an alarm function.

A contemporary automatic alarm
watch, made by Maurice Lacroix, is worth
looking out for because of the scarcity
value of mechanical alarm wristwatches.

THE MOONPHASE

The moonphase indicator on a watch dial
can turn the banal into the special. Some of
the movements linked to the indicator can
be quite simple, merely showing a rotating
moon which can be set more or less
accurately. Others will take into account
the lunar month, showing the twenty-nine
and a half days with the various phases of
the moon positioned accordingly.

ABOVE EL PRIMERO: MOONPHASE CHRONOGRAPH BY ZENITH WITH AN
18 CARAT GOLD CASE, PART OF A CONTEMPORARY LIMITED EDITION.

ABOVE CONTEMPORARY QUARTZ CHRONOGRAPH BY DUNHILL, INCLUDING A CALENDAR MOVEMENT.

CALENDAR MOVEMENT

A proper calendar movement does not just indicate the date; in general it comprises day and date, month and, perhaps, a moonphase. A quartz calendar movement will normally be programmed to take into account the different lengths of the months, but an automatic one will not be unless it is a perpetual (a self-winding automatic) movement. It is important to ensure that the displays for the day/date/month are correctly synchronized; if not, the information will be incorrect. The information is displayed by one of three methods: dial or windows or a combination of both.

The first perpetual calenders are thought to have appeared around 1853. A perpetual calendar movement takes up where the ordinary calendar movement leaves off. This movement should require no adjustment for leap years, thanks to a complicated system of wheels and satellite wheels or bearings, generally linked to the month display.

QUANTIÈME PERPÉTUEL

The feature known as *quantième perpétuel*, which is linked to a calendar or perpetual calendar function, indicates the ability of the watch to adjust itself to the specific number of days in each month. Again, the term relates just to mechanical watches.

PERPETUAL CALENDAR

The perpetual calendar wristwatch sometimes comes with a year indicator on the face. This is a window and not a dial to avoid confusion of another hand.

GRANDE COMPLICATION

Only attempted by the very few, the *Grande Complication* is a combination of minute repeat, chronograph, and perpetual calendar movements. A piece with this kind of movement is a collector's item even before it leaves the drawing board.

Although the case will be made of the most precious of metals, this is one of the few instances where the movement is infinitely more valuable than the case. *Grandes Complications* first appeared in the second half of the nineteenth century and seem to have originated in the Vallée de Joux, near Geneva which was then, as now, the center of the Swiss watchmaking industry. The wristwatch versions of the *Grande Complication* movement were first produced in the late 1980s, but they are

ABOVE THE BEAUTY OF THE TOURBILLON MOVEMENT IS SEEN THROUGH THE BACK OF THIS JAEGER-LECOULTRE REVERSO.

sought after by international collectors and are probably not the easiest pieces for the amateur collector to find. Blancpain has produced a *Grande Complication* which includes a *tourbillon* and a split-second chronograph (stopwatch).

THE TOURBILLON

The *tourbillon* is held to be the brainchild of Abraham-Louis Breguet, who applied for the patent in February 1798. It forms part of a mechanical watch's movement and relates to the accuracy. It is found only on watches of superlative quality.

The power from the mainspring is controlled through the escapement, the balance wheel, and the balance spring. The pull of gravity when the watch is worn can adversely affect the rate of the movement so the balance wheel and escapement are enclosed in a cage mounted on a pivot. This cage actually rotates on itself, generally once a minute, to correct any shift in position caused by outside movement, thus keeping the rate constant.

Such a sophisticated mechanism tends to make the watch more expensive. However, from a collector's point of view, it is worth the investment. Such are the difficulties involved in the manufacture of a *tourbillon* that only the large, prestigious watch houses will attempt it: Blancpain, Jaeger-LeCoultre and Girard-Perregaux, for instance. Jaeger-LeCoultre have produced a Reverso with a *tourbillon*, thus combining the beauty of a Reverso case with all the sophistication of the *tourbillon* movement.

IMPORTANT AMERICAN MANUFACTURERS AND THEIR WATCHES

BULOVA
Accutron, 1960–76; Excellency range 1920s and 1930s; doctor's watch, *c.*1930; Charles Lindbergh Lone Eagle watch, 1927

ELGIN
Lady's convertible wristwatch, 1912; soldier's watch, 1917; Art Deco ladies' watches, 1928/9

GRUEN
Doctors' watches, 1920–40s; Curvex General, 1932; The Varsity, 1933

HAMILTON
Enamel bezel watches, 1920s; Seckron doctor's watch, 1936; Electric Model 500, 1957; Everest Electric, 1958; Thin-O-Matic, 1963

ILLINOIS
Started 1905; joined with Hamilton 1927; produced quality watches with offbeat designs

INGERSOLL
The first character watch – Mickey Mouse, 1933; Dan Dare and Jeff Arnold watches, 1960

WALTHAM
Pierced case soldiers' watches, 1917–19; twenty-year Gold-Filled, 1917; baguette models, 1931

DESIGNS OVER THE DECADES

Longines Lady's Watch

DATE *1915*
MATERIALS *18 carat white gold
with diamonds*
SPECIAL FEATURES *Engraving
around the dial*

After the quiet elegance of the Edwardian era came the "Roaring Twenties" and Cubism. Its dynamic influence was felt throughout the home, spreading into the sphere of personal adornment and accessories, and watches were not left out. The style was meant to reflect the new liberalism and to leave behind the stifled ideas of the previous age. The idea that a utilitarian object could be good to look at was firmly implanted in people's minds and influenced the design of everyday wristwatches. Handsome pieces were no longer reserved for the privileged few and prices were made more accessible, thanks to advances of mechanization on early assembly lines.

Yellow Gold Lady's Bracelet Watch

DATE *1928*
MATERIALS *Yellow gold*
SPECIAL FEATURES *The movement is very small and the bracelet is slim and elegant*

Outside influences have touched watch design in much the same way as everything else. As you become more absorbed in the study of watches, you will soon find that you are often able to date a piece just by glancing at it, as it reflects the style of its particular time.

Early designs were usually linked to either wars or sports and they tend to have a much heavier look about them, reflecting the style of the pocket watch from which they are the direct descendants. As the new technology was first of all mastered and then perfected, movements were created for finer and finer cases. Finally, small, elegant ladies' pieces, such as this bracelet watch, were made feasible.

THE 1930s

The 1930s signaled the end of Prohibition and a new fluidity to the old structures of the previous decade. Surrealism was now the buzz word and, at the same time, the person on the street began to show an interest in sporting activities. Watches for golf, such as the Reverso by Jaeger-LeCoultre, date from the beginning of the 1930s. Whereas men's watches were becoming more "masculine" in looks to complement their new outdoor lifestyle, watches for ladies' evening wear were growing smaller and more delicate in design, reflecting the new fashions.

An examination of the advertising of the era shows that manufacturers were trying to promote the idea of one watch for each activity or part of the wearer's life – one for sports, one for dress occasions, and one for casual and office wear. This is probably because the techniques that were needed to make the more delicate-looking watches strong enough to withstand tough sports wear were simply not available at that time and the cases for the more elegant styles could not take the pressures of vigorous physical activity.

Pour vos courses, au printemps, prenez une LONGINES

Rendez-vous de chasse et de sport vous imposent une LONGINES

ABOVE ADVERTISEMENTS FOR WATCHES FROM THE 1930S.

Lady's Jaeger-LeCoultre Reverso

DATE *1932*
MATERIALS *18 carat gold*
SPECIAL FEATURES *The original models were mechanical*

When the first Monsieur LeCoultre settled in the Vallée de Joux during the sixteenth century, having fled persecution by the Catholics, little did he realize that he was founding a famous dynasty. Antoine LeCoultre opened up his own watchmaking factory in 1833 in a place called Le Sentier. Today Jaeger-LeCoultre movements and cases are still produced by hand in Le Sentier.

The Reverso was first produced in 1931 and is still made today. Combining the beauty and purity of line of the era of its conception with the strength necessary for sportsmen and women of the time, the Reverso, with its ability to pivot on itself to get out of harm's way, was a truly unique classic in every sense.

Man's 1920s Chronograph (Longines)

DATE *1920s*
SPECIAL FEATURES *Round dial in a square, curved case. The crown contains the chronograph button*

Longines produced several ranges of classic collectibles and one of the most interesting was the Lindbergh range which commemorated the 1927 crossing of the Atlantic by Charles Lindbergh in his aeroplane, the *Spirit of St Louis*. This event gave birth to the Lindbergh collection in 1933 and the original sketch for this wristwatch was actually made by Lindbergh himself.

Longines watches are renowned for their durability and strength, as can be demonstrated in the excellent example featured here.

Jaeger-LeCoultre Calendar Watches

DATE *1940s*
SPECIAL FEATURES *Both watches show the date using an extra red-tipped hand*

Classically timeless and highly collectible, the house of Jaeger-LeCoultre has traditionally been responsible for many of the "firsts" in watch design. In 1847 LeCoultre et Cie produced the first keyless watch mechanism, replacing the key with a crown winder on the side of the case.

Although not strictly to do with watch-making, the "almost perpetual motion" Atmos Clock was also the brainchild of Jaeger-LeCoultre. This unique timepiece is powered by minute temperature differences: there is no key or electric impulse. The Calender Watches shown above are another clever design, with the added facility of an extra hand which shows the date.

Jaeger-LeCoultre Mysterieuse

DATE *1945*
MATERIALS *White gold and diamonds*
SPECIAL FEATURES *The small single diamond is the minute indicator and the larger one shows the hours*

During World War II all manufacturers' efforts were directed towards the supply of combat forces, and civilians were generally expected to make do with utility goods or with pre-war products. As a result, there are few watches, other than military, dating back to this period. A few attractive jewelry pieces, such as the Mysterieuse, still exist. Note the small size of this watch, which is an indication of the difficulties experienced by the manufacturers in finding suitable quality materials. Some watch companies of the time actually stopped making timepieces during the war years, instead supplying small machinery parts to the various government agencies. Others restricted their manufacturing to very plain and unornamented versions and on straps rather than on metal bracelets.

The Mysterieuse

DATE *1948*
SPECIAL FEATURES *As the big watch houses dared to move away from the austerity imposed by the Second World War, more unusual designs began to evolve*

After years of austerity and with more materials readily available and a redistribution in wealth as the blue-collar class in both Great Britain and the USA grew in size, designers were setting their stamp on everything from table lamps to motor cars. Watch design in those first post-war years slowly gained momentum and became more adventurous and, with workshops now freed from wartime production, innovative movements like The Mysterieuse, which was created by Jaeger-LeCoultre, began to appear.

Longines Lady's Watch

DATE *1940s*
MATERIALS *Diamonds and 18 carat white gold*
SPECIAL FEATURES *An elegant, tapered watch case that is set with diamonds*

This beautiful evening watch is typical of the range of classic collectibles produced by Longines. Although rather delicate in appearance, this watch is quite durable and strong. The Longines company later went on to produce the classic quartz movement watches, which were revolutionary in that they could be guaranteed an accuracy of twelve seconds per year, an achievement even for quartz.

Cartier Man's Strap Watch

DATE *1960s*
SPECIAL FEATURES
Stylized dial

As can be seen from the design of this Cartier watch, Pop Art was just around the corner and a more daring approach was taken by the

high-profile brands of watch. Every design concept in the Sixties seemed to be "sturdy." Gone were the delicate ladies' watches of previous decades and colors were used in profusion: turquoise, coral, and amethyst all featured strongly.

Lady's Cartier Watch

DATE *1970s*
MATERIALS *Gold watch on a leather strap*
SPECIAL FEATURES *Note the Cubism influence from the early 1970s*

During the late 1960s and the 1970s great progress was made in both style and exterior visual appeal of watches. This may have been due to the fact that Swiss watch manufacturers were having to compete against the wave of Far Eastern digital watches which were starting to flood the international market. This was an era of contrasts: budding consumerism on the one hand and rapidly growing environmental awareness on the other. The arrival of quartz led to revolutions in the trade.

The developing youth culture in the late 1970s and early 1980s meant a rediscovery of consumer goods and the advent of the "yuppie" culture, which led to an increasing demand for good-quality watches of fashionable design, such as those produced by Cartier.

Rado's Diastar 48

DATE *1973*

SPECIAL FEATURES *This was the first quartz model from the Diastar range, showing the company's interest in unusual case materials*

Throughout the 1970s fashion houses and watch companies themselves brought out new lines to keep up with the styles dictated by the catwalk. The fashion houses themselves had very little part in the manufacture of these watches except to insist on stringent quality control.

The advent of quartz led to a revolution in the watch trade and extremes in design resulted from the earlier Op and Pop Art influences. There was also an increasing demand for good-quality fashionable watches amongst consumers.

Omega Watch

DATE *1973*

MATERIALS *Silver bracelet and amethyst crystal*

SPECIAL FEATURES *This particular watch won the Rose d'Or Design Award*

In the 1970s designer watches, such as those created by Omega, began to appear in force to satisfy a label-hungry public and fashion houses such as Christian Dior, Yves St Laurent and Gucci all had watches specially designed to complete their particular "look" for the season. These pieces were generally made with gold-plated cases and Swiss watch movements. Designer watches indicate the changing fashions through this decade and can make an interesting collection.

Lady's Rodolphe Watch

DATE *1980s*

SPECIAL FEATURES *Created in the era of "power dressing," this watch is smart and chic with a highly individual dial*

Technological excellence was not enough in the 1970s; the product had to look good as well as being functional in order to compete in a more and more crowded marketplace. Fashion-conscious pieces were brought out at prices previously reserved for the fairly conservative design lines. This classically stylish watch is typical of the time.

Gucci Designer Watch

DATE *1970s*

SPECIAL FEATURES *This particular model from the House of Gucci has a series of interchangeable bezels*

The watches that were commissioned by the fashion houses of the 1970s can make an interesting collection: as they were meant to have high fashion appeal, the colors and materials employed may be slightly more adventurous than those used by the true watch houses. The bezels on this Gucci watch were interchangeable which meant that the wearer could coordinate the watch with the rest of their wardrobe.

Rado Art Watch

DATE *1990s*
SPECIAL FEATURES *Note the perfect integration of the bracelet into the watch case*

In the early 1990s sports watches maintained their popularity, but there was an increase in models falling into the middle ground between sports and dress areas and some sports pieces even showed a few diamonds! The interest in reviving old designs had not died out and copies of earlier watches remained extremely popular, either as true replicas or by taking the original design as the basis for a new version of the idea.

This watch by Rado crosses the fine line between art and watch design, which first began to evolve in the late 1940s with work from the American artist, George Horowitz, who was a follower of the Bauhaus movement.

Longines Art Watch

DATE *1952*
MATERIALS *Enamel dial*
SPECIAL FEATURES *This early art watch has an astral theme on the dial*

The Bauhaus school was one of the major influences on art watch design. This movement applied the theory that machine-inspired aesthetics could be used for everyday objects. One of the leading artists, George Horowitz, still has designs that are available today, including the famous plain black dial with a single gold dot marking twelve o'clock. Since then several artists have been asked to design a specific piece or to grant permission for one of his/her works of art to be incorporated into a new creation.

Beautiful designs, such as those produced by Longines, make spectacular additions to any collection, but they are extremely sought after by enthusiasts.

Andy Warhol's Times/5

DATE *c.1988*

SPECIAL FEATURES *Five separate movements and five different views of New York*

The Movado watch company has made a point of commissioning watches as works of art from several major contemporary artists. One in particular, who made a sizeable contribution although he died before its completion, was Andy Warhol, with his Times/5 wristwatch. It comprised five different photographs of New York as individual dials and five separate watch movements were unique to this piece. It was made in a limited edition of 250; 50 pieces were retained by Movado and 200 went on sale in 1988 for $18,500 each.

James Rosenquist's Elapse Eclipse

DATE *1991*

SPECIAL FEATURES *Designed to mark the eclipse of 1991, the presentation case carries over the theme introduced by this watch*

In 1991 James Rosenquist presented Elapse, Eclipse, Ellipse. This featured several watches – this time three – with mechanical movements, made of silver and with a dark blue leather strap decorated with silver stars. The creation of this piece followed the artist's works entitled Welcome to the Water Planet: one blue dial, Ellipse, represents the earth as seen from outer space; Eclipse represents a meteor; and finally Elapse is an abstract concept of time. The piece is packaged in a pyramid-shaped box, which was an integral part of the whole design concept.

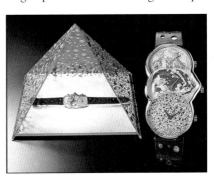

JEWELRY WATCHES

Cartier Lady's Strap Watch

DATE *1913*
MATERIALS *White gold and diamonds*
SPECIAL FEATURES *The size of stones above and below the watch case make this an important piece*

Often a watch is the only type of personal jewelry that some people will wear and it is important that it suits their personality and lifestyle. As can be seen from this splendid example by Cartier, it does not have to be plain and uninspiring, since such a range of materials is available for watch cases. Stones can be set in the case, dial, bezel or bracelet to turn an ordinary wristwatch into a dazzling piece of jewelry. The type of cut used on the stones should be examined to help value the watch. When buying a jewelry watch, always check the quality of the movement: they were often inexpensive to begin with and may not have survived in good working order.

Strap Watch

DATE *Unknown*
MATERIALS *White gold and diamond-set*
SPECIAL FEATURES *The dial is entirely set with diamonds, leaving none of the dial plate visible to the eye*

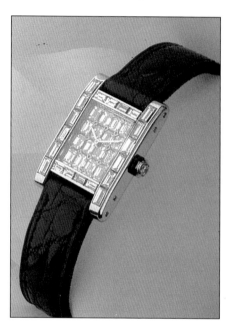

Where diamonds have been used in a watch, the quality of the setting and the color of the gems are important if the watch is very heavily gem set, just as in the case of any piece of jewelry. The type of cut used on the stones should also be examined to help value the watch and to date it. Where the diamonds are tiny, a simple eight-sided cut is understandable, but if the watch has larger stones, they should be of good quality, color and cut.

Omega Jewelry Watch

DATE *1925*
MATERIALS *Platinum case and bracelet*
SPECIAL FEATURES *The watch is set with a large sapphire and eighty-two diamonds*

A good way to check the setting on an older watch is to hold it next to your ear and to shake it gently – any loose stones will rattle slightly. Matching up a lost stone of unusual cut or color can be time-consuming so any damage to the jewels must be considered when discussing prices. Watches on bracelets, such as this example, lend themselves perfectly to embellishment with gemstones and there are endless permutations. The case shape may vary from the usual round or square form and may even be heart-shaped, a half-circle or perhaps a totally abstract non-geometric form.

Jaeger-LeCoultre Watch

DATE *1950*
MATERIALS *Leather strap with diamonds*
SPECIAL FEATURES *Diamonds are set outside the dial as hour markers*

The beauty of the jewelry watch is often related to the thickness of the case and the way in which it may curve to follow the line of the wristbone. Today most examples of this type of watch are fitted with a quartz movement and sapphire glass; they cannot be made very water resistant due to their construction. On older pieces water resistancy may not have been a feature initially, so it is important to treat this type of watch with great care. This unusual 14 carat gold watch from Jaeger-LeCoultre works well for everyday and evening wear.

Jean Lassale Watch

DATE *Unknown*
MATERIALS *18 carat gold with leather strap*
SPECIAL FEATURES *This watch was dedicated to Gilda and to Rita Hayworth who portrayed her in the film of the same name. The 18 carat gold chain is wrapped around a leather strap*

Jean Lassale is a relative newcomer to the jewelry watch scene. Since 1975, when the company laid claim to the slimmest watch in the world, it has received numerous prizes, awards, and medals, but in 1985 it thrust itself forward with the Thalassa range, featuring highly stylized watches with models for men and women, showing the artist's interest in design.

The Jean Lassale Company decided that a watch must be an object of beauty, and functional, so giving pleasure to the wearer. With ranges such as La Passion, it is not surprising that these watches have a unique appeal.

Raymond Weil Watch

DATE *Unknown*
MATERIALS *Gold-plating with crystal*
SPECIAL FEATURES *Raymond Weil's personal technique of gold plating makes this spectacular piece suitable for everyday wear*

The development of extra-slim quartz movement watches in the mid-1970s made jewelry watches more accessible and opened out new design possibilities. New companies with fresh ideas were founded as a result and one of the most successful was Raymond Weil. His Othello collection with an 18 carat gold electro-plated extra-slim case, with either a plain black dial or set with Austrian crystals, marked a new standard for middle-of-the-range jewelry pieces. This collection contained the slimmest quartz movement available in that price range. It paved the way for Raymond Weil's first solid gold and diamonds wristwatch, the Parsifal, carrying on the concept of elegance which has been the company's trademark.

Man's Longines Wristwatch

DATE *1960s*
MATERIALS *Gold*
SPECIAL FEATURES *Engraved automatic movement in two colors*

This engraved wristwatch from Longines was produced in very limited quantities, so making it a collector's piece. Jeweled watches, like this one, were among the first wristwatches and stones from the days before modern grading and cutting often show subtle differences which can only add to the overall character of a piece.

On older pieces, but this also applies to later designs, water resistancy may not have been an original feature: for example, pieces fitted with quartz movement and sapphire glass cannot be made very water resistant because of their construction. It is important that the wearer treats this kind of watch with the care such valuable items deserve.

Piaget Jewelry Watch

DATE *Unknown*
MATERIALS *Rubies and diamonds*
SPECIAL FEATURES *The dial is pave set*

This is an important stone-set piece from the House of Piaget, which contains rubies and diamonds. The company makes influential jewelry pieces for both sexes. Its use of high-quality stones and the availability of the same piece with more or fewer gems allow a flexibility in the price range of these watches.

Jennifer, Scheherazade and Stella Watches

DATE *Unknown*
MATERIALS *18 carat gold and stone set*
SPECIAL FEATURES *Stella has a gold accessory clip set with diamonds and rubies*

One general misconception about jewelry watches is that they need to be rather conservative. This has been disproved over recent years by younger companies like Jean Lassale, who created the watches shown opposite, which have unique appeal.

The Stella model is a strap watch which forms part of an accessory clip set with diamonds and rubies. A company whose early efforts included a watch called Mata Hari can perhaps only be expected to continue with named models such as Scheherazade, and pieces which use lapis lazuli, diamonds, rubies, and emeralds. Jean Lassale has also recently launched a boxed set of "his and hers" watches, known as the California range.

Piaget White Gold and Diamonds

DATE *c.1960s/1970s*
MATERIALS *White gold and diamonds*
SPECIAL FEATURES *Note the use of striking colors in this design*

The House of Piaget is renowned for its use of high-quality stones, as demonstrated in these stunning pieces. This is an excellent range for the collector to watch out for, as the range of jewelry pieces for both sexes is important to the history of jewelry-making. Look for pieces that are similar in design, but with more or fewer gems to vary the style.

Lady's Chronograph

DATE *Unknown*
MATERIALS *18 carat gold with diamonds*
SPECIAL FEATURES *Unusual diamond-set chronograph with an 18 carat yellow gold case*

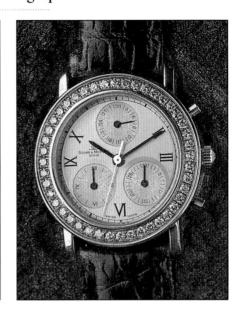

Baume et Mercier, who designed this watch, specialize in perhaps more delicate-looking jewelry pieces, including some beautifully crafted loose-link bracelets. These are often attached to their watch cases with gem-set gold. Both brands have shown a good availability in 18 carat white gold, which is somewhat unusual, but demonstrates the company's strong understanding of public taste.

These pieces are important and collectors should keep a look-out as they are becoming more and more sought-after.

Piaget Stone-Set Dials

DATE *Unknown*
MATERIALS *Turquoise, malachite, and lapis lazuli*
SPECIAL FEATURES *High-quality stones*

One of the most important features of designs from the House of Piaget is the use of high-quality stones. The same (or similar) design is often available in a variety of stones, as shown here as well as in 18 carat white gold, which is unusual. These watches are striking and original, with a flexibility in the price range which makes them ideal for collectors. Simple leather straps in coordinating colors do not detract from the beauty of the stones.

Ocean 2000

....

DATE *Unknown*
SPECIAL FEATURES *Porsche designed diver's automatic watch with water resistancy to 6,560 ft and ratchet bezel*

The ratchet bezel on this watch allows for specific timing, for example, when diving. On all good watches this bezel is unidirectional so that, in the case of a blow to the watch in which the bezel is moved, diving or flying time (for instance) is shortened, not prolonged.

The seals on water resistant watches should be checked intermittently, especially when they are used in salt water, which corrodes the inner sealing ring. Note that chronograph cannot be activated or de-activated under water. This excellent example of a sporting watch comes from the International Watch Company.

Breitling Chronomat

....

DATE *Unknown*
SPECIAL FEATURES *Slide-rule used by pilots before the age of flight computers*

Breitling is well known for its specialist sports watches. Many of the older and heavier models are still in existence, some of which have links with important aviation events and with air forces all over the world. The Chronomat is Breitling's most famous watch and is available in many different guises. The automatic version has a diving bezel and is water resistant. Breitling also produces the Cosmonaute, a watch for the serious pilot, which has a slide-rule bezel and a twenty-four hour movement (as seen here).

Parsifal Chronographs

DATE *Unknown*

MATERIALS *18 carat gold*

SPECIAL FEATURES *When sports meet jewelry in a range called Parsifal*

These two splendid watches shown above are by Raymond Weil and prove that sports watches do not have to be ugly or ungainly in appearance. Many watches, such as these, are surprisingly good-looking, but are able to maintain the ability to withstand normal sports wear and tear. These watches are available in stores today both as current lines and as past successes.

Cartier Sports Watch

DATE *1990s*
SPECIAL FEATURES *Revolutionary chrono-reflex movement*

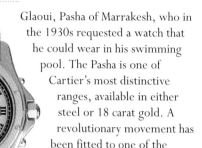

The chrono-reflex feature is an ingenious system for indicating the number of years to go until a leap year, as well as the date, the month, and the hour according to the twenty-four hour clock.

The Diablo is one of a range of sports watches from Cartier and this great name first unveiled its Pasha range in 1985, named after El Glaoui, Pasha of Marrakesh, who in the 1930s requested a watch that he could wear in his swimming pool. The Pasha is one of Cartier's most distinctive ranges, available in either steel or 18 carat gold. A revolutionary movement has been fitted to one of the Pasha series, so that it is not just a chronograph, but also a calendar watch. The case is amazingly small, especially when the number of functions is taken into consideration.

Contemporary Girard-Perregaux Wristwatches

DATE *1990s*
MATERIALS *Steel and 18 carat gold*
SPECIAL FEATURES *Classic sports watch design examples*

Girard-Perregaux has applied its many years of experience to the production of both classic and sports chronographs and also offers a range of diving watches called Sea Hawk which would satisfy the most exacting collector. The classic good looks of its GP 4900, one of the few watches available in pink gold, are reminiscent of an earlier age, while the company's commitment to the future is very clearly demonstrated in the clean and sober lines

of its GP 7000 series. In production since 1990, again using both yellow and pink gold, GP 7000 is a range of watches with sapphire glass and automatic movements.

Breitling Navitimer

DATE *Unknown*

SPECIAL FEATURES *Attractive utilitarian piece from a range designed with specific sports in mind*

The flagship chronograph of the Breitling company is the Navitimer, which is still produced today by the original factory in Grenchen, Switzerland. The precision and ease with which crucial information is made legible is probably one of the main reasons that Breitling timing instruments have claimed an important position on the instrument panel of many a legendary aircraft, such as the Boeing Clipper and the DC3, and you will often see retired employees of the company wearing their official-issue Breitling.

Breitling Automatic Chronograph

DATE *Unknown*

SPECIAL FEATURES *Water resistant to 330 ft*

The chronograph shown below is from the famous Chronomat range produced by Breitling. This model has been specially created for divers. Breitling are a company who cater particularly for the needs of specialist sportsmen and women: there is even a Breitling Yachtmaster in the range, which has an automatic chronograph movement and five- and ten-minute warning zones.

LONGINES

Since 1867, when Ernest Françillon opened the Longines factory, the company's name has been linked to major sporting events, with the commitment to precision timing that this entails. A manufacturer of marine chronometers needing to withstand the rigors of journeys to the Arctic and the Antarctic (not the least famous of these expeditions was led by Captain Bernier, when he navigated from the USA to the North Pole on his ship, *The Arctic*), as well as producing watches for sports from motor racing to cycling, Longines has been directly involved in great sporting events throughout the twentieth century.

ABOVE LONGINES CONQUEST CHRONOGRAPH. PRODUCED TO COMMEMORATE THE XX OLYMPIC GAMES IN MUNICH IN 1972.

Omega Pilot's Watch

DATE *1934*

SPECIAL FEATURES *Revolving bezel with an arrow index for determining flight duration*

The first Omega Speedmaster was taken to the moon in 1969 because you can't have an automatic movement in the absence of gravity! Precision of these chronographs was so good that it enabled the crew of one space mission to make crucial calculations to establish navigational positions when contact with Earth was broken. The design has remained basically the same, but has been constantly improved and updated by the company. Omega's latest venture has been to introduce a titanium and rose gold

Seamaster with a water resistancy of 1,000 ft and a ratchet diving bezel. This pilot's watch is a good example from the Omega range.

Omega Seamaster

DATE *1970s*

SPECIAL FEATURES *Water resistant to 6,560 ft*

Omega first introduced designs that could be used underwater in 1934 and the company has solved the problem of helium gas release in a new way. Instead of having an open valve, it has perfected a screw-down crown at ten o'clock which can be opened when and if needed, letting out any helium while preventing water from seeping in.

This particular design was used by Commander Jacques Cousteau for a series of experiments at 1,640 ft underwater.

Tag-Heuer Formula I Chronograph

DATE *1990s*

SPECIAL FEATURES *This particular version is a contemporary classic among sports watches*

It would be impossible to collect sports watches and ignore the importance of Tag-Heuer. Tracing its history back to 1860 and being the official timekeeper at the 1920 Olympics, Tag-Heuer has made a remarkable comeback since the early 1980s, when it had all but slipped out of sight. In 1985 the link between the watch manufacturer Heuer and the group TAG (Techniques d'Avant Garde) was made and Tag-Heuer has forged ahead ever since. Obviously any piece that you come across with only the name Heuer on the dial pre-dates 1985.

Most of the Tag-Heuers of today have a quartz mechanism,

ensuring the precision demanded by competing sportsmen and women worldwide. Edward Heuer's interest in technological achievement led to many patents, the first very early on in the company's history, being for a new system of water-sealing cases. The company's efforts were not limited to the field of watches alone: its considerable expertise was also put to use in the making of car dashboard timers, and in 1942 it launched the Solunar, which showed the ebb and flow of the tides and indicated the times when fishing would be particularly good! Today the Tag-Heuer factory is still in a position to service most pieces bearing the old Heuer brand, be they mechanical or quartz. Automatic Tag-Heuers are rare and much sought after.

Contemporary Rolex Submariner

DATE *1990s*
MATERIALS *Available in steel, yellow metal and steel, and 18 carat gold*
SPECIAL FEATURES *Model No. 16610*
Water resistant to 1,000 ft, rotating bezel

One of the most famous diving watches of all time must surely be the Rolex Submariner, with an automatic movement, chronometer certificate and water resistance to 1,000 ft. It is beaten only by another Rolex product, the Sea Dweller. Perfectly capable of submerging to a depth of 4,000 ft, this is, incidentally, the only Rolex with a date that does not have a magnifying bubble. The Sea Dweller has been produced solely in steel, whereas the Submariner has been produced in steel, yellow metal and steel, and also in 18 carat gold.

Omega Speedmaster Professional

DATE *1960s*
SPECIAL FEATURES *Chosen by NASA in 1965 for moon and space missions*

This piece was first launched in 1946 and any design model without the name "Professional" pre-dates 1965. To commemorate the twentieth anniversary of the important date 20th July 1969, Omega produced a limited edition of 2,500 stainless-steel Speedmaster professional chronographs, each inscribed with the words "Apollo XI 1969" on the edge and bearing on the back "The first watch worn on the moon" and "Flight qualified by NASA for all manned space missions." It is worth remembering that the precision of these chronographs was so good that it enabled the crew of one space mission to make crucial calculations to establish important navigational positions when contact with earth was broken.

41

MILITARY WRISTWATCHES

IWC Pilot's Watch

DATE *1940*

SPECIAL FEATURES *Fitted with a pocket-watch movement, this watch was meant to be worn over a flying suit*

Generally speaking, a pilot's wristwatch will have a center second hand, while an infantryman's or ordinary foot soldier's watch may have a second hand dial just above the six on the watch face. Pilots' wristwatches also tend to be a little larger, so that they can be strapped to the leg and used as navigational tools, when needed. IWC still make military pieces today.

Omega Military Wristwatches

DATE *1917*

SPECIAL FEATURES *The wristwatch on the far left was issued to the US Signal Corps*

Military wristwatches, such as these by Omega, have very interesting features, but they also have important historical connections which can again be used as the basis for a collection. Some enthusiasts collect only World War II infantry wristwatches, for example.

Omega are still producing some of their original designs (as are Jaeger-LeCoultre and some companies specializing in military supplies). Before making a purchase, however, check that you are buying a genuine military wristwatch and not just a souvenir piece.

World War I Zenith Land and Sea Wristwatch

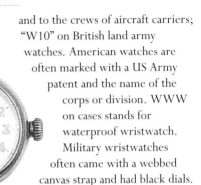

DATE *1916*
MATERIALS *Solid silver*
SPECIAL FEATURES *This wristwatch was probably owned by an officer*

Marking on the case backs of military wristwatches will give a clue as to whom they were issued and for what purpose. "6B" may be found on pieces issued to the British RAF and to the crews of aircraft carriers; "W10" on British land army watches. American watches are often marked with a US Army patent and the name of the corps or division. WWW on cases stands for waterproof wristwatch. Military wristwatches often came with a webbed canvas strap and had black dials.

British Pilot or Aircrew Watch/British Army Wristwatch/ CWC British Service Issue

DATES *1942–52/1969/1987*

Wristwatch (1) is a British Pilot or Aircrew watch with Air Ministry markings 6B/195 A32024. It was manufactured by Omega throughout 1942–52. Center (2) is a 1969 wristwatch that was made for the British Army by Smiths which made both quartz and mechanical watches. Finally, wristwatch (3) is a CWC British service issue wristwatch that has been fitted with a Swiss quartz movement.

43

Cartier Wristwatch

DATE *1927*
SPECIAL FEATURES *From design to finished product, a classic such as this never shows its age*

A classic watch is made up of a combination of factors: durability of style and design, and a certain understated elegance, plus strength of case and reliability of movement to withstand years of daily wear. Since 1847 the name of Cartier has been synonymous with outstanding quality. The company is responsible for some of the most beautiful jewelry ever seen, and has translated its experience of incredibly high standards into the delicate art of watchmaking. The House of Cartier has produced countless pieces, each more beautiful than the last and, for many reasons, collectors' items in their own right.

Rado Diastar

DATE *Unknown*
SPECIAL FEATURES *The use of modern materials contributes to the creation of new classics*

Some watch houses have specialized more than others in the production of classic lines. They have been making the same basic designs for years, perhaps with slight variations in the dial or movement. These pieces, such as the Rado Diastar, have achieved their reputation over a length of time, proving their strength, durability and the company's refusal to cater for passing fads.

Lines are generally manufactured for a number of years, discontinued, then reintroduced with slight variations to continue the original theme. It can be extremely interesting to locate the original of a particular range and to follow it through to the present day.

Santos by Cartier

DATE *1930s*

SPECIAL FEATURES *Presented on a leather strap. Today's models are more usually sold on a bracelet*

Cartier was supplier to the Imperial Court of Napoleon III, and Les Must de Cartier was launched in 1973 to continue that special tradition of quality. These were a range of items starting with watches,

but continuing with pens, lighters, perfumes and so on, that was more a definition of lifestyle than a production of a series of utilitarian objects. Les Must de Cartier watch range has been continued from that date using the same basic case design, either rectangular or circular, but with the periodic introduction of a new dial.

Classic Cartier Tank

DATE *Unknown*

MATERIALS *18 carat gold*

SPECIAL FEATURES *The simplicity of the case is well set off by the leather strap*

The Cartier Tank is a basic design that exists in many forms. Cartier's design team has really shown, over the years, what can be done with the basic Roman numeral dial, while still maintaining the tradition of quality and this is what makes Cartier such a great name. For instance, the numerals can be enlarged so that they virtually join in the center, or they can be placed down the side of the case.

Cartier Jeweled Strap Watch

DATE *Unknown*
MATERIALS *Diamonds*
SPECIAL FEATURES *Note the unusual diamond-set design on either side of the case*

This stunning example from the House of Cartier is a true classic. A watch such as this one could be worn for many years and still remain pleasing and contemporary in its appearance.

Lasting style often equals simplicity of design and purity of line; anything too fussy will probably not remain to your taste throughout the years to come.

The classic pieces from this watch house have achieved international recognition as their fame and collectibility are quite highly prized among collecting enthusiasts.

Contemporary Vacheron Constantin

DATE *Unknown*
SPECIAL FEATURES *The bi-colored dial adds to the clarity of the face*

A variation on a classic line from Vacheron is typical of the classics that all reputable watch houses continue to produce. These usually consist of a strap watch with a plain gold case and either a white dial with black numerals or a champagne dial with baton markers, and are available in versions for both men and women. These lines are manufactured for many years, discontinued, then reintroduced with slight variations to continue the original theme. It can be interesting to locate the original of a particular range of watch and then subsequently to follow it through to the present day.

Royal Oak by Audemars Piguet

DATE *Available since early 1970s*
SPECIAL FEATURES *This particular model is available in a variety of materials*

From its earliest years Audemars Piguet established itself as a manufacturer of complicated movements. In 1920 it was responsible for the smallest repeater watch, measuring ⅝ in, in diameter.

In 1972 came the Royal Oak, named after three Royal Navy battleships which were themselves named for Charles II's famous hiding place after his defeat by Cromwell. The design succeeds in emphasizing both simple and complicated movements, and its pinnacle was achieved with the automatic *Quantième Perpétuel* first produced in 1984 and much sought after as a major collector's item since that date. Not only does the Royal Oak design set off some of the most beautiful movements, it also lends itself to production in many different metals, ranging from the traditional watchmaking materials to that newcomer to the industry, tantalum.

Contemporary Blancpain Quantième Perpetuel

DATE *Unknown*
MATERIALS *18 carat yellow gold*
SPECIAL FEATURES *The watch can adjust itself to the specific number of days in each month*

Since 1735 there has never been a quartz Blancpain and there never will be – such is the motto of the Blancpain house and indeed, in 1735 when Jehan-Jacques Blancpain founded his original watch-making enterprise high up in the Jura Mountains, he established himself as a perfectionist. All Blancpain pieces still carry the undeniable stamp of craftsmanship which is visible at a glance; each order is the personal responsibility from beginning to end of an individual watchmaker, who personally signs the piece when it is finished.

The Blancpain workshop, which is housed in a former farmhouse, is about as far from an assembly line as you can possibly get.

Jaeger-LeCoultre Reverso

DATE *1931*
SPECIAL FEATURES *A perfect example that shows exactly why this design has become one of the most famous classics and it is still available today*

Antoine LeCoultre opened up his own watchmaking factory in 1833 in Le Sentier and today movements and cases are still being produced by hand at the same site.

The House of Jaeger-LeCoultre has traditionally been responsible for many "firsts." For example, in 1847 LeCoultre et Cie produced the first keyless watch mechanism, replacing the key with a crown winder on the side of the case. The Reverso was first produced in 1931 and is still made today. It combines beauty and purity of line with the necessary strength for the sportsman or woman to wear. With its unique ability to pivot on itself to get out of harm's way, this is a true classic in every sense and has been so right from the beginning.

Contemporary Dunhill

DATE *c.1980s*
SPECIAL FEATURES *Note the elegance of classic lines*

Not all watch brands that have enjoyed lasting popularity belong to a traditional watchmaking or jewelry firm. The company of Alfred Dunhill, for example, that very English purveyor of luxury goods, has, since it was started at the beginning of this century, produced very fine pieces which still attract considerable attention today. Their most famous designs include the Vermeil (1975), the Millennium range (1982), the Elite (1986) and the Limited Edition Dress Watches.

Longines Watch

DATE *Late 1940s*
MATERIALS *18 carat gold*
SPECIAL FEATURES *Tear-drop shaped horns*

Since 1867 when Ernest Françillon opened the Longines factory, Longines has produced whole ranges of classic collectibles, the most notable being the Lindbergh. These watches are known for their durability and strength. Another of the company's successes was the Conquest range, a very sports-orientated design, but slim and elegant enough to rate as a classic. It comprised a quartz movement, revolutionary in that it could be guaranteed an accuracy of twelve seconds per year, an achievement even for quartz.

Longines Lindbergh Watch

DATE *1933*
MATERIALS *18 carat gold*
SPECIAL FEATURES *This unique design was first thought of by Lindbergh himself*

The most notable range from Longines was Lindbergh, which commemorated the 1927 crossing of the Atlantic by Charles Lindbergh in his aeroplane, the *Spirit of St Louis*. This event gave birth to the Lindbergh collection in 1933 and the original sketch for this wristwatch was by Lindbergh himself.

Longines Watch

DATE *1940s*
MATERIALS *9 carat gold*
SPECIAL FEATURES *Rectangular case and unusual grooved horns that cover the strap attachment*

A rare classic from the 1940s by Longines. This slim and elegant watch is prized by collectors and it is well worth searching for these pieces even if a little tenacity is required to locate a particular model. The fame and collectibility of works from Longines is renowned throughout the world as they have a strong commitment to precision.

Hand-Wound Omega

DATE *1967*
SPECIAL FEATURES *This was one of the first designs from the Omega Company's De Ville range*

Omega has produced a number of collectible ranges over the years, including not only the classic and ongoing De Ville range, but also the more adventurous Constellation. For the more experienced collector, Omega's Louis Brandt range, all automatic, comprises of a perpetual calendar, a chronograph and a plain automatic movement in 18 carat gold on leather straps. This range was exclusively produced to celebrate the company's founder, Louis Brandt (1825–79).

Rolex Perpetual Datejust

DATE *Unknown*

MATERIALS *Steel and yellow metal with sapphire glass*

SPECIAL FEATURES *Model No. 16233 with screw-down crown: a classic suitable for sportswear*

Rolex did not confine itself to the production of sports or sports-orientated watches. In 1931 a patent was granted for the Perpetual mechanism, thanks to which, in 1945, the Rolex Datejust became the very first wristwatch with a date display on the watch face. Again, taking the idea further proved to be no problem for Rolex, and in 1956 the Day-Date was launched. It is uncertain which Rolex model is the most collectible, from the earliest cushion shapes to the well known Datejust. For many people, Rolex pieces represent the climax of the fine art of watch-making and, even for the non-connoisseur, their general image is one of the absolute ultimate in luxury and desirability.

Gold Rolex Oyster

DATE *1927*

MATERIALS *9 carat gold*

SPECIAL FEATURES *One of the first waterproof gold watches*

Hans Wilsdorf, a name remembered by all watch lovers, was the founder of the Rolex watch company in 1905. By 1910 Rolex had obtained the first ever chronometer certificate awarded to a wristwatch. The firm worked extremely hard to improve the strength of wrist-watches which were, at that time, rather prone to damage by dust and humidity. By 1926 it was conducting tests which involved immersing an individual watch in water for about three weeks, and in 1927 Mercedes Glietze swam across the English Channel wearing a Rolex Oyster watch. The company had at last found the solution to the problem of making a watertight case with the invention of the screw-down crown in what was, for Rolex, the successful beginning of a whole series of waterproof watches, each guaranteeing water resistance to unheard-of depths.

Modèle avec Personnages (GZ100) / Millepattes (GZ103) / Serpent (GZ102) / Blanc sur Noir (GZ104)

DATES *1986*
SPECIAL FEATURES *Extra-flat movement of ²⁄₂₅ in thick*

The Swiss watch industry suffered badly in the late 1970s and this spurred on the Swiss Corporation for Microelectronics and Watchmaking Industries Ltd to come up with the first Swatch – the Delirium. These watches called for a movement that was as inexpensive as possible, designed to fit into a plastic case.

It took three years of intensive planning to produce waterproof, shock-proof and accurate watches such as these examples, all made from synthetic materials with a low production cost. The first Swatch was launched in 1983.

Swatch Jelly Fish

DATE *1983*
SPECIAL FEATURES *This was one of the first Swatch Specials*

From the spring of 1984 all Swatches produced were given a personal name as well as an individual number, and with the first Swatch Specials on the market, the serious collecting of Swatches may be said to have truly begun. The first Swatch Special was the original Jelly Fish (1983), and this was closely followed by the 1984 Olympic Specials.

Black Puff/Havana Puff/Royal Puff/Petrol Puff/Cardinal Puff

....

DATE *1988*

SPECIAL FEATURES *This series was entitled "Blow your time away"*

One of the most remarkable Specials, but a series this time, was the Puff series, which had as its theme "Blow your time away." This was the 1988 Christmas Special. As an indication of its popularity, when a store was set up in London's Covent Garden for one day and allocated 1,000 pieces, overnight Swatch enthusiasts formed a queue and by 4:00 pm the store had nothing left to sell.

Christmas Specials are a facet of the Swatch story. There are Swatch Chronographs, Scuba Swatches, Maxi Swatches, Art Swatches, Swatch Automatics, and "Swatch Musicall," a musical alarm Swatch by Jean Michel Jarre.

Vivienne's Pop Swatch

....

DATE *1992 Fall/Winter PWK 168 Putti*

SPECIAL FEATURES *This watch was specially commissioned and created by Vivienne Westwood*

If you collect Swatches, the permutations are endless. Not only have they produced limited editions, specials and singles, but also whole series by major contemporary artists: for instance, the Pop Swatch Art Series, One More Time, by Alfred Hofkunst, which comprises three models. The firm's first art watch (which has recently been sold at auction for a very large sum of money) was the 1985 Kiki Picasso. This was followed in 1986 by a series by Keith Haring featuring four pieces. The year 1987 was represented by the Folon Series together with Tadanori Yokoo. In 1988 there was the Foundation Maeght Series by artists such as Pol Bury, Valerio Adami and Pierre Alechinsky. Before embarking on a search for such elusive pieces, it may be more practical to set your sights a little lower and concentrate on some of the early singles.

Zoo Loo, Chicchirichi (GR112)

DATE *1992*
SPECIAL FEATURES *Cartoon Cockerels*

From the start Swatch proved that it was much more than just a frivolous fun watch. It showed that Swiss technology and expertise could be used for something visually exciting to all age groups which would also be inwardly as reliable and as sturdy as one of the heaviest stainless-steel sports watches.

If you become a Swatch collector, you will be joining a worldwide club with over 130,000 members. Its own newspaper, *The Swatch Journal*, transmits information to members as speedily as possible. Members are offered special Swatches not sold through normal outlets. The company also publishes a yearly catalog to bring them up to date on the four annual launches: spring, summer, fall, and winter.

Jelly Fish Chronometer (GK 100)

DATE *1990*
SPECIAL FEATURES *The certificate that was issued with this Swatch makes it even more of a collector's item*

Swatch put itself to the test and produced a run of 4,843 Swatches which were issued with chronometer certificates. These pieces were submitted to a whole range of tests, including freezing temperatures, 90-degree humidity and, being left for twenty-four hours on a vibration machine. Obviously, with just an issue of only 4,843 pieces worldwide, Swatch Chronometers do not often appear on the market, but their very existence is proof of testing.

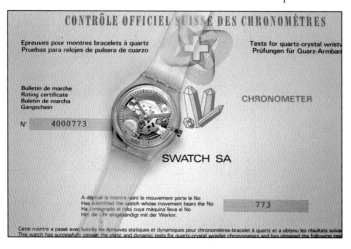

Swatch Chronograph Signal Flag (SCN 101)

DATE *1990*

SPECIAL FEATURES *Four stepping motors, but the same size case*

The year 1990 saw the arrival of the Swatch Chronograph, a highly sophisticated movement with four stepping motors yet with a case the same size as that of the ordinary Swatch. Then the watch became available with a leather strap in 1991. The Swatch Chronograph offers functions to record finishing time and intermediate time and a tachometer for speed indication. Early chronographs are much sought after and should form part of any Swatch collection. The company has gone further with the Stop Swatch: the first push on the button sends the hands back to twelve o'clock and another push starts a stop watch with a six-hour range.

Christmas Hollywood Dream (GX 116)

DATE *1990*

SPECIAL FEATURES *This Swatch is one of a range of Swatch Specials issued by the company*

The Swatch creators did not set out to start a trend, but Swatch mania has prevailed since the early days, and each new product launched has been greeted with such enthusiasm that, in some cases, supply has been far outstripped by demand. The reasons behind all this are simple enough – Swatch has an excellent product selling for the right price and a marketing team capable of taking it into realms so far not thought of by anyone else. Moreover the watch's bright colors and affordability appeal to younger people, its reliability attracts the purist who wants a highly precise timekeeper, and the sportsperson is also catered for with the chronographs and diving watches. Finally, because Swatch's popularity has snowballed (even in the art world, thanks to the Art Specials like the Hollywood Dream, above), there are now models kept in glass cases in museums – which, for a watch which started out as an inexpensive "second watch," is truly an amazing achievement.

GALLERY OF WRISTWATCHES

A S YOUR INTEREST in the subject of wristwatches grows, you may wish to look out for certain pieces that can really make a collection, such as a 1930s Duoplan by Jaeger-LeCoultre, a fabulous creation from Cartier (if you wish to spend serious money!), or even an interesting contemporary watch such as those produced by Swatch, which are already limited editions and can only increase in value and interest to collectors over the coming years. Whatever your choice, you will find plenty of ideas to inspire you over the following pages.

LEFT LONGINES AUTOMATIC CONQUEST FROM THE 1960S. THIS MOVEMENT IS UNUSUAL IN THAT IT HAS A POWER RESERVE INDICATOR IN THE CENTER OF THE DIAL.

ABOVE THIS WATCH IS MORE THAN FIFTY YEARS OLD, BUT THE CLEANLINESS OF THE MOVEMENT SHOWS THAT THE PREVIOUS OWNERS HAVE TAKEN GOOD CARE OF IT, MAKING IT A SAFE PURCHASE.

RIGHT CONTEMPORARY MINUTE REPEATER BY BLANCPAIN IN 18 CARAT YELLOW GOLD. THE OVERALL SIMPLICITY HIDES A VERY SOPHISTICATED MOVEMENT.

ABOVE LIMITED EDITIONS ARE NORMALLY INDICATED ON THE WATCH ITSELF. FOR EXAMPLE, THIS PIECE IS NO. 15 OUT OF A TOTAL PRODUCTION OF 300.

BELOW WHEN BROWSING THROUGH STORES AND AUCTION HOUSES, BE ALERT: THIS INNOCENT-LOOKING BANGLE HAS AN EARLY ROTARY WATCH CONCEALED ON THE INSIDE.

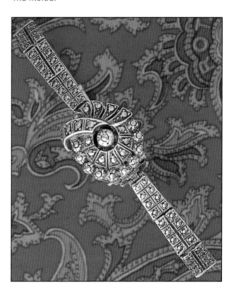

LEFT AND RIGHT TWO JEWELED AUTOMATIC MOVEMENTS. THE JEWELS ARE CAREFULLY POSITIONED IN BOTH PIECES FOR MAXIMUM EFFICIENCY.

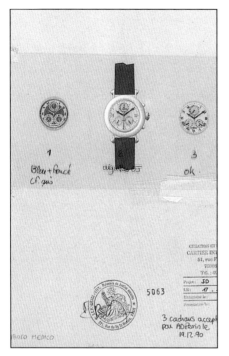

ABOVE FOR GREAT HOUSES SUCH AS CARTIER, EACH DESIGN IS CAREFULLY NUMBERED AND REGISTERED FROM THE INITIAL CONCEPT TO THE FINISHED PRODUCT.

BELOW VERY EARLY CARTIER WRISTWATCH ON A SATIN STRAP. THE TIME WAS MEANT TO BE READ WITH THE WRIST HELD STRAIGHT UP RATHER THAN ACROSS THE BODY.

LEFT 9 CARAT GOLD ROLEX DRESS WATCH WITH GOLD BRACELET FROM THE 1930S.

ABOVE EARLY LADY'S CARTIER WRISTWATCH WITH A
PEARL BEZEL. PEARLS ARE FAIRLY RARE ON WATCHES.

RIGHT ANOTHER VERY
EARLY CARTIER
WRISTWATCH FOR LADIES.
THE "BOOTLACE" STRAP IS
TYPICAL OF THE PERIOD
(*c*.1926).

LEFT A STAINLESS STEEL, MIDI SIZE, ROLEX OYSTER *c.*1940–45. THIS WATERPROOF WATCH WAS PATENTED IN 1925.

ABOVE CARTIER WATCH COMBINING CALENDAR, MOONPHASE AND CHRONOGRAPH.

ABOVE LARGE CHRONOGRAPH ($1^{21}/_{32}$ X $1^{21}/_{32}$ IN) PRODUCED BY LONGINES IN THE LATE 1960S. THIS MODEL HAS THE PECULIARITY OF ENABLING CALCULATIONS OF TENTHS OF A SECOND.

ABOVE OMEGA COSMIC MOONPHASE, 1947: THE
FIRST OMEGA CALENDAR WATCH INDICATING
SIMULTANEOUSLY THE EXACT TIME (DATE, DAY, MONTH)
AND MOONPHASE.

BELOW BREITLING AEROSPACE,
STANDARD ISSUE TO THE RAF'S
RED ARROWS. THIS WATCH IS IN
THE COMPARATIVELY NEW METAL
TITANIUM.

ABOVE WATER RESISTANCY IS AN IMPORTANT
FEATURE OF MOST SPORTS WATCHES. THIS MODEL BY
TISSOT IS WATER RESISTANT TO 330FT.

ABOVE 1933 ADVERTISEMENT SHOWING THE
STRENGTHS OF OMEGA SPORTS WATCHES.

ABOVE THE COLOR OF TIME BY ARMAN, A 1990
LIMITED EDITION BY MOVADO.

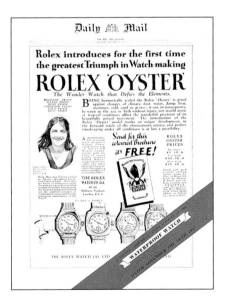

ABOVE ROLEX'S FRONT-PAGE ADVERTISEMENT FOR
THEIR OYSTER WRISTWATCH PATENTED IN 1925.

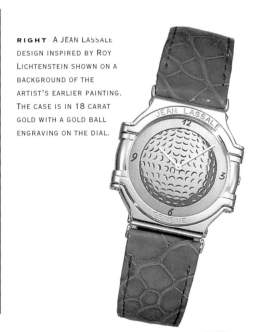

RIGHT A JEAN LASSALE
DESIGN INSPIRED BY ROY
LICHTENSTEIN SHOWN ON A
BACKGROUND OF THE
ARTIST'S EARLIER PAINTING.
THE CASE IS IN 18 CARAT
GOLD WITH A GOLD BALL
ENGRAVING ON THE DIAL.

ABOVE CONTEMPORARY DUNHILL WATCH. THE DESIGN SHOWS THE RENEWED INTEREST IN OLD STYLES.

ABOVE 1930S DUOPLAN BY JAEGER-LECOULTRE, THE WATCH WITH AN ACCURACY OUTSTANDING EVEN IN THE 1990S.

LEFT THE SIZE OF THESE TWO OMEGA MOVEMENTS (BAGUETTE ON THE RIGHT, OVAL ON THE LEFT) COULD BE ACHIEVED ONLY WITH QUARTZ TECHNOLOGY.

LEFT WHAT MAKES A WATCH INTERESTING IS A COMBINATION OF DESIGN, TECHNOLOGY AND HISTORY. ON THE RIGHT IS PICTURED A RARE OMEGA ANTIMAGNETIC FROM 1925 WITH BREGUET HOUR MARKERS. ON THE LEFT IS A 1940 CHRONOGRAPH WITH UNUSUAL DIAL COLORING TO DISTINGUISH THE VARIOUS FUNCTIONS.

ABOVE SUCH WAS THE SUCCESS
OF THE MEMOVOX THAT JAEGER-
LECOULTRE CARRIED THE DESIGN
OVER WELL INTO THE 1960S. THIS
ONE IS HAND-WOUND AND WAS MADE
IN 1964.

LEFT THESE EARLY DUNHILLS
REVEAL THE POPULARITY OF THE
RECTANGULAR CASE IN THE FIRST
PART OF THIS CENTURY.

ABOVE ONE MORE TIME: GU (H) RKE PWZ 100.
BONJU (H) R PWZ 101 AND VERDU (H) RA PWZ
102, POP SWATCH ART, 1991.

TOP RIGHT 700 YEARS
SWISS CONFEDERACY, FLACK
(GZ 117) BY NIKLAUS
TROXLER, SWATCH ART,
1991.

RIGHT YURI (GG 118),
IGORTS SWATCH, 1992,
FALL/WINTER.

ABOVE THE TWO SWATCHES SHOWN IN FULL ARE THE SDK 100 DEEP BLUE SDN 400 BORA BORA AND SWATCH SCUBA 200, 1990/1991.

ABOVE TADANORI YOKOO (GZ 107, RORRIM 5), SWATCH ART, 1987.

RIGHT 700 YEARS SWISS CONFEDERACY, 360 DEGREES (GZ 119) BY ROSSO SU BLACKOUT, SWATCH ART, 1991.

BELOW 1990 SWATCH
CHRONOGRAPH. THIS MODEL WAS AN
IMMEDIATE SELL-OUT WHEN IT WAS
FIRST INTRODUCED.

ABOVE FOUNDATION MAEGHT SERIES: GZ 110 BY
POLBURY, GZ III VALERIO ADAMI AND GZ 401 BY
PIERRE ALECHINSKY, SWATCH ART, 1988.

ABOVE LADY LIMELIGHT AND SIR LIMELIGHT
(LB 110 AND GB 106), 1985.

ABOVE SWATCH CHRONOGRAPHS
1990/91:
1 SANDSTORM (SCB 104)
2 SKIPPER (SCN 100)
3 SKATE BIKE (SCB 105)

TIPS FOR COLLECTORS

IT IS IMPORTANT to keep an open mind when bidding for a particular watch. Do not forget that you may not be the only person interested in it, and never stay in the bidding for longer than you mean to! Local taxes and auction house charges (generally between 10 and 15 percent) are added on top of the price reached in the bidding. This should be kept in mind to avoid nasty shocks when it comes to paying for your purchase.

As a collector, you will want to keep your collection alive. One way to do this is to use part-exchange as a method of purchase: many dealers and retailers will make an allowance for this. If you have decided that a wristwatch, for whatever reason, does not belong in your collection, put it to one side for part-exchange with another.

MAKING A GOOD PURCHASE

Once you have decided where to buy and what to buy, there are a few points to remember when purchasing a vintage wristwatch. If you are going to wear the watch, it must be capable of telling the time; if not, it must be returned to working order. With a quartz watch, it may be a matter of replacing the battery, but a service and overhaul may add to your overall outlay in purchasing a watch.

ABOVE THESE LONGINES WATCHES ARE INTERESTING BECAUSE OF THE DEVICE THAT BLOCKS THE OUTER BEZEL TO ALLOW FOR ACCURATE ADJUSTMENT OF THE TIME.

If a mechanical wristwatch is not in working order, there could be a multitude of reasons. If a ticking sound can be heard when the watch has been wound but the hands are not moving, it is possible that the hands have come away from the dial train (the wheels and pinions of a watch).

If there is complete silence, if the watch cannot be wound or if there is a "grinding" feel when you try to wind it, things could be serious and the possible repair costs must be taken into account when considering purchasing the watch.

THE IMPORTANCE OF
DOCUMENTATION

When you buy a new watch, you should be issued with the appropriate box, a valid guarantee, a full set of instructions matching the movement of the watch (unless the operation of the watch is so basic that you do not need instructions) and, most important of all if the watch has the word "chronometer" on the dial, you should be given the certificate proving that it has passed the most stringent chronometer testing.

When purchasing a second-hand item, remember that the more valuable and rare the item, the more documentation will add to its value. The original guarantee, stamped by the original retailer, together with the right box can add a great deal of money to the asking price.

Whether buying old or new, beware of the difference between a limited edition and a special edition. In principle it is easy to remember. As part of a limited edition for which only a relatively small number of watches have been produced, the watch will carry a number: this number is individual to the watch. A special edition will possibly be a commemorative piece or a production tied to some sporting event, with no set number but with, perhaps, a note as to the commemoration on the back of the watch face.

HOW TO CARE FOR
YOUR COLLECTION

Mount your collection of wristwatches on rolls made of soft fabric or acid-free tissue paper, if they do not have their own boxes.

Never leave dead batteries in quartz watches. If a mechanical wristwatch stops, get it serviced straight away. Find a good watch repairer early in your collecting career and stay with him or her – you will learn a lot.

Your collection will need cleaning from time to time. This refers to the outside only: never attempt to clean, oil or regulate the movement or change the battery yourself, but always leave any dealings with the inside of a watch to the professional watch repairer. To clean the case of most metal watches, use a soft cloth. Certainly never use solvents on gold plate or silver gilt. Silver watches may be rubbed gently with an appropriately impregnated cloth. If the water resistancy has been confirmed, the metal part of a wristwatch may be cleaned in soapy water and dried with a soft fiberless piece of fabric.

CHECKING FOR DAMAGE
BEFORE BUYING

Examine the watch with a magnifying eyeglass. Do not forget to check the strap or bracelets well: if you are buying the watch to wear, it will not stay on your wrist for long if the pins (lugs) are bent or if the stitching, in the case of a leather strap, is worn.

Although several grades of leather are used for straps, the most water resistant being sharkskin, you are not likely to find the original leather on a vintage watch. The finer the watch, the better the grade of leather the strap would have been initially. However, be it boarskin, ostrich skin, calf, crocodile or lizard, if you wet a leather strap on a regular basis it will deteriorate quicker, and the harder you intend to wear the watch, the stronger the strap needs to be. In fact, for frequent sports use, a metal bracelet is best.

One problem to look out for with metal bracelets is stretching. If the links seem far apart with large gaps between them and a lot of "play," the bracelet needs professional attention. If it is made of gold, the metal may have become worn and the lugs inside the links may be worn or distorted.

A watch with a machine-made gold bracelet will be less expensive than one with a mainly hand-assembled loose-link type. The problem likely to occur with these machine-made bracelets after a number of years is splitting: this can be repaired by a goldsmith.

COLLECTING THEMES

Alarm watches
Car watches
Design styles, e.g. Art Deco
Designer label watches
Early digitals
Jewelry watches
Limited edition watches
Mechanicals
Military watches
Mystery watches
Novelty watches
Reversos
Skeletons
Sports and hobbies watches
Swatches
Watches with bangle bracelets
World timers

FURTHER COLLECTING TIPS

ORGANIZING YOUR COLLECTION

Each piece in your collection should have its own file containing its photograph, the date and place of purchase, any important serial and model numbers and information regarding related pieces. The photograph will be invaluable should it become necessary to insure all or part of the collection, and serial numbers can help trace a provenance. This file should contain guarantees or chronometer certificates issued by the manufacturer.

LEFT SIGN OF THE TIMES: IN THIS 1930S ADVERTISEMENT FOR AN OMEGA SPORTS MODEL, THE WATCH WAS PROMOTED AS BEING SUITABLE FOR SPORTSMEN, SAILORS AND "COLONIALS!"

LEARNING MORE ABOUT WATCHES

In addition to books on wristwatches, there are also collectors' magazines which provide detailed information about featured models. When you visit a watch retailer, do not forget to ask for the current catalogs of any brand that takes your interest. Much can be gained from having a small, well-ordered library of such literature, including news releases, historical facts, details of technological improvements and so on. It can also be interesting to ask the auction houses for their sale-room catalogs after an auction, with a list of prices achieved: this will keep you up to date on desirable prices and give you some idea of the current value of your own collection.

COLLECTING BY THEME

Most "young" wristwatch collections represent a mixture of styles, manufacturers and themes. As your collection grows and you learn more about the subject and what you do and do not like, your purchases are likely to become more specialized and the watches will fall naturally into categories or themes which you can then expand upon. The themes are varied and you should not be restricted.

CHILDREN'S WATCHES

An interesting – and less expensive – collection can be formed from novelty and children's watches. The first watch specifically aimed at children was made in 1933 by Ingersoll and featured Mickey Mouse; since then a wide range of images and designs have been introduced.

ABOVE DINOTIME AND FANTASEA WATCHES FOR CHILDREN BY FLIK-FLAK. THESE ARE WATER RESISTANT WATCHES MADE FROM RECYCLED MATERIALS WITH APPEALING DESIGNS.

Flik-Flak, a Swiss company, has an excellent range which is ideal for starting a collection. Young children are well catered for with Flik-Flak's teaching watches, and the company also offers a good range of pictorial models featuring dinosaurs and seahorses. The watches are made from recycled aluminum, have a canvas strap and can be machine-washed at 104°F!

There is also a large selection of character watches featuring well known faces through comics, cartoons, popular television shows, films, and computer games. An interesting collection could be formed by tracing the changing image of an old favorite, such as Bugs Bunny, through the decades.

Do not forget that children enjoy collecting. There are many modern, brightly colored and inexpensive wristwatches to suit the younger pocket. Researching and looking after a collection is fun. Children take delight in swapping, which can be useful when the pocket money runs out.

GLOSSARY

ANALOG Time indication by hands and dial; means "corresponding." Originally an electronic term, which was adopted by watchmaking with the spread of the quartz watch.

ANTIMAGNETIC WATCH Watch whose parts are protected from all but the very strongest magnetism; quartz watches cannot be disturbed by the phenomenon.

APPLIED NUMERALS Raised metal characters attached to the dial.

ARABIC NUMBERS 0, 1, 2, 3, 4, 5, 6, 7, 8, 9. Originated in India and introduced by the Arabs to Europe in about the tenth century AD.

AUTOMATIC WATCH Mechanical watch with a mainspring that is wound by the wearer's movements, via a rotor. It was invented by Abraham-Louis Perrelet in the eighteenth century; Breguet called his self-winders "perpetuelle."

AUXILIARY DIAL A small dial showing seconds only, up to one minute, usually at the six o'clock position.

BACK WINDER Flat crown set into the back of the case for setting time and winding.

BAGUETTE Rectangular movement, with a length at least three times its width. Popular shape for Art Deco watches.

BALANCE Running regulator of mechanical watch; it oscillates about its axis of rotation, the hair-spring making it swing to and fro ("tick-tock") in equal time parts. Balances of modern wristwatches beat up to ten beats per second.

BARREL Circular box housing mainspring; teeth attached at edge drive gears; going barrel has great wheel mounted upon it.

BATON NUMERALS Undecorated non-numerical markers of hours, minutes and seconds.

BEZEL Metal surround frame in which watch glass (crystal) is fitted.

BREGUET HAND Popular design by Breguet; the slightly tapered needle of the hand ends in a pointed head mounted on a circle, which is pierced with a hole. Sometimes called a moon hand.

BUTTON Better known as a crown, or winder; sometimes refers to a chronograph.

CABOCHON CROWN (WINDER) Crown or winder set with a jewel.

CALIBER Once used only to denote the diameter of a watch movement; now often only indicates type (e.g. man's, lady's, automatic). Generally given with manufacturer's name. From Latin *qua libra?* (of what weight?), or from Arabic *kalib* (mold, i.e., circumference, measurement, scale).

CARAT The official scale by which the purity of the gold is determined. Pure gold is 24 carat; 18 carat is alloy in which 18 parts in 24 are gold; 14 carat contains 14 parts of gold and so on. Also used as the unit of weight for precious stones.

CASE The housing for movement, dial and glass.

CHRONOGRAPH Watch which also has an independent stopwatch for short interval timing. Common types of chronographs are one-button (using crown, or separate button above it); two-button (the most common, the top button stopping and starting the time-measuring function and the bottom one resetting it); twelve-hour with moonphase; split-second.

CHRONOMETER Ordinary watch which has passed extremely severe precision and reliability tests in an official (generally Swiss) observatory (e.g. Neuchâtel).

COMPLICATED WATCH Watch with functions not related directly to the time of day. For example, calendars, chronographs, moonphases, perpetual, repeaters, etc.

CROWN Knob, generally positioned outside the case at three o'clock, for winding, correcting and setting.

CRYSTAL Glass dial cover (in fact made of glass, plastic, synthetic sapphire or quartz crystal), fitted into bezel. Plastic scratches; glass (common in pre-1940s watches) shatters easily; sapphire glass is virtually scratch-proof.

DEPLOYMENT BUCKLE Two strips of hinged metal (curved to the wrist shape) on the watchband; upon closing, one folds over the other to cover it. Probably invented by Cartier.

DIAL Face of watch, showing hours, minutes, and seconds. Other small dials are called subsidiary dials.

DIVER'S WATCH Water resistant.

DOCTOR'S WATCH Also known as a duoplan or duodial. An auxiliary seconds dial is separate from the hour and minute dial; useful for quick reference when taking a pulse count.

FORM WATCH Watch in any very unusual shape.

GOLD Yellow, pink or white, used for both cases and bracelets.

HACK FEATURES (BALANCE STOPPING) Second hand which is stopped to synchronize time, when the crown is pulled out.

INTEGRAL BRACELET Designed as a natural extension of the watch case.

JEWELS Used as bearings at points of greatest friction in movements; commonly fifteen to eighteen are used (the quantity is not indicative of either quality, or value of watch). Formerly, natural rubies and sapphires were used; today most such jewels are synthetic.

LUG Part or parts of watch case to which band, bracelet or strap may be attached.

MAINSPRING Principal spring in watch; a flat spring is coiled in a barrel.

MEAN TIME Average length of all solar days in year; the usual time shown by watches.

MINUTE REPEATER Repeating watch that sounds hours, quarters, and minutes.

MONTH APERTURE Pierced window in a mechanical digital watch displaying month, often abbreviated.

MOONPHASE WATCH Watch displaying phase of moon through twenty-nine and a half days (correction for extra forty-four minutes per month often incorporated).

MOVEMENT Complete mechanism of watch; from 120 to more than 600 parts may be incorporated in it.

OYSTER CASE Rolex watch with water resistant case.

PAVE Literally "paved with," as in dial with precious stones.

PERPETUAL Self-winding automatic watch (see also AUTOMATIC WATCH).

PERPETUAL CALENDAR Calendar mechanism with display which automatically corrects for long and short months and leap years. Formula adjustments for vagaries of the Gregorian calendar continue only until 28 February 2100; that is not a leap year, so manual changes will have to be made to all but the most complicated watches; likewise 2200, 2300, 2500, 2600 and 2700 will not be leap years.

PLATINUM Precious silver-white metal, which is heavier than gold. Used for both cases and bracelets.

QUARTER-REPEATER Repeating mechanism which sounds hours and quarter hours.

QUARTZ Rock crystal (silicon dioxide) that can be made to oscillate by electronic switching, maintaining its very constant frequency, in accordance with its cut. Synthetic quartz crystals are used today.

ROLLED GOLD   An extremely thin sheet of hot gold, pressed on to another metal; gold on watch cases is usually double thickness.

ROMAN NUMERALS   Besides Arabic, the most common numerals used on watch dials; note IIII instead of IV.

ROTOR   In automatic watches, the rotor winds the mainspring; in quartz watches, it is a permanently rotating magnet in the step-switch motor.

RUBY   The "ruby" referred to in watchmaking today is, in fact, corundum, a synthetic stone. It is used to reduce wear on certain pivots.

SAPPHIRE   Glasses (crystals), sold as scratch-proof, are made of synthetic sapphire.

SHOCK-RESISTANT WATCH   A watch is held to be shock-resistant if, when dropped on to a hardwood surface from a height of 3 ft it does not stop, or if its daily rate does not change by more than sixty seconds.

SIGNED MOVEMENT   The signature on a movement of its maker, which is likely not to be the same as that on the dial.

SKELETON WATCH   The dial of a skeleton watch has a separate chapter ring with the interior cut away, leaving only numerals and exposing the wheels and the interior mechanisms of the movement. The back plate is also cut away and fitted with glass.

SPLIT SECOND CHRONOGRAPH   Chronograph with sweep second hand, independent of chronograph hand.

STEM   Shaft connection between winding mechanism and crown on outside of case.

SUBSIDIARY DIALS   Smaller auxiliary dials, which show elapsed minutes and running seconds.

SWEEP SECONDS (CENTER SECONDS)   Second hand mounted at dial center and extending to chapter ring.

"SWISS MADE"   A Swiss Federal government ordinance dated December 23, 1971 decrees that this expression can only be featured on a watch and used in connection with its marketing if (a) at least 50 percent of the components, by value, excluding costs of assembly, are of Swiss manufacture, (b) it was assembled in Switzerland, (c) it was started up and regulated by its manufacturer in Switzerland, and (d) it is continuously subject to the legal obligation of technical inspection in Switzerland.

TACHOMETER   Speedometer or revolution recorder on bezel.

TANK CASE   Today, the common name for a rectangular case; originally, exclusive name of Cartier wristwatch.

TONNEAU   Case shape with wide center and flat tapered ends.

TOURBILLON   Invention by Breguet for nullifying vertical position errors by means of a revolving platform which goes through all such positions, so that they neutralize each other.

TRITIUM   Luminous paint used for dials, hands, and numerals.

TUNING FORK   A transistor continually switching between two small magnets to regulate smooth running, oscillating 360 times a second. The high frequency gives great precision in time-keeping. Bulova Accutron made the use of the device famous, but then quartz watches usurped its popularity.

WATER RESISTANT   Expression for "water-proof," which is illegal in the USA. Water resistant watches, sold as such, must be able to withstand water pressure at a depth of 3.28 ft for 30 minutes and thereafter for 90 seconds at 65.6 ft. Divers' watches, in fact, have much greater resistance.

WORLD TIME WATCH   A watch that can be made to depict current time in any chosen city or zone, according to the model.

FURTHER INFORMATION & ADDRESSES

BRITAIN

The Antiquarian Horological Society, New House, High Street, Ticehurst, East Sussex TN5 7AL

Bonhams, Auctioneers, Montpelier Street, Knightsbridge, London SW7 1HH

British Horological Institute, Upton Hall, Upton, Newark, Nottinghamshire NG23 5TE

Christie's, Auctioneers, 8 King Street, St James, London SW1Y 6QT

Phillips, Auctioneers, Blenstock House, 7 Blenheim Street, New Bond Street, London W1Y 0AS

Sotheby's, Auctioneers, 34-35 New Bond Street, London W1A 2AA

International Watch Magazine, Hyde Park, 5 Manfred Road, London SW15 2RS

USA

Christie's, Auctioneers, 502 Park Avenue, New York NY 10022

National Association of Watch and Clock Collectors Inc., 514 Poplar Street, Columbia, Pennsylvania 17512-2130

Sotheby's, Auctioneers, 1334 York Avenue, New York NY 10021

The Time Museum, 7801 East State Street, PO Box 5285, Rockford, Illinois 61125-0285

SWITZERLAND

Christie's, Auctioneers, 8 Place de la Taconnerie, 1204 Geneve

Musée d'Horlogerie, Chateau des Monts CH-2400 Le Lod

Musée d'Horlogerie et de l'Emaillerie, Route de Malagnou 15, 1208 Geneve

Musée International d'Horlogerie, Rue des Musées 29, La Chaux-de-Fonds

Sotheby's, Auctioneers, 13 Quai de Mont-Blanc, CH 1201 Geneve

Swiss Watch and Jewelry Journal, International Edition, 25 Chemin du Creux-de-Corsy

A CHRONOLOGY OF
WRISTWATCH INVENTION

19TH CENTURY	1900–09	1910–19	1920–29	1930–39

1838
Louis Audemars
invents stem winding
and setting mechanism

1868

Patek Philippe makes
the first wristwatch

1871
Aaros Dennison of the
International Watch
Company (IWC)
invents the waterproof
watchcase

1880
Girard-Perregaux
produces a wristwatch
for officers of the
Imperial Austrian Navy

1888

Cartier produces a
lady's wristwatch with
diamond and gold
bracelet

1902

The first Omega
wristwatch is produced

1902
93,000 wristwatches
sold in Germany

1903
Louis Brandt, founder
of Omega, dies

1904
One of the most
famous early
wristwatches appears –
the Santos-Dumont
produced by the House
of Cartier

1910
Longines begins
wristwatch production

1911
Santos-Dumont
wristwatch goes on
general sale

1912
Movado makes an army
wristwatch with a
protective grid over the
glass

1914
First alarm wristwatch
is made by Eterna

1917
British Royal Flying
Corps issued with
wristwatches by Omega

1918
Omega supplies US
Army with
wristwatches

1920

Audemars Piguet
produces the smallest
repeater watch ($^5/8$ in)

1923
Invention of the
automatic wristwatch
by John Harwood (the
prototype is made by
Blancpain)

1925
Patek Philippe
produces the first
wristwatch with a
perpetual calendar

1927
First water resistant
Rolex Oyster produced

1930
Smallest lady's watch
movement to date –
baguette shaped – is
produced

1930
Tissot develops the first
antimagnetic
wristwatch

1932
Launch of Reverso by
Jaeger-LeCoultre

Manufacture of the
Lindbergh Aviator by
Longines (to the design
of Charles Lindbergh)

1933
First watch for children
made by Ingersoll
(featuring Disney's
Mickey Mouse)

Longines made official
timekeeper at the
Brazilian Grand Prix

1936
Omega appointed
official timekeeper for
the Olympic Games

78

1940–49	1950–59	1960–69	1970–79	1980–89

1940–49

Hamilton supplies US forces with wristwatches; Omega and Breitling supply RAF watches during the war years

1945
Rolex Date/just is the first watch with a date display on the watch face

1946
Audemars Piguet produce the thinnest wristwatch in the world ($\frac{1}{15}$ in)

1947

American Nathan George Horwitt designs the Movado Museum Watch

1950–59

Poljot, the first Russian wristwatch, is produced – later to become Sekonda

Tissot develops Tissot Navigator, a self-winding wristwatch with a universal calendar

Rolex Submariner goes down 1,000 ft

1952
Breitling introduce the Navitimer, a super chronograph designed especially for pilots

1953
Lip's battery-powered watch is introduced

1957

Hamilton produces the first electric watch

1960–69

1960
Bulova launches Accutron, the electronic tuning-fork watch invented by Max Hetzel

1966
Girard-Perregaux produces the first high-frequency mechanical watch (36,000 vibrations per hour)

Creation of Betal I, the first Swiss quartz movement

1969
Girard-Perregaux develops the first mass-produced quartz watch

International Watch Company introduces the Da Vinci wristwatch

Longines produces the first quartz cybernetic wristwatch

Zenith brings back the El Primero, the epitome of chronograph movements

Neil Armstrong wears an Omega Speedmaster Professional on the moon

1970–79

1972
First stainless-steel luxury wristwatch is made (Audemars Piguet)

1972
Longines launches an LCD (liquid crystal display) watch

1975

Launch of Raymond Weil brand, with innovative ultra-slim movement

1976
Launch of Maurice Lacroix brand

1978
Vacheron Constantin Kallista is sold for $5,000,000

1980–89

1983
Swatch is launched

Rolex Sea Dweller goes down to 4,000 ft

Longines launches the Conquest range, accurate to about one minute in five years

1985

Tag-Heuer brand appears on the market

1986
Tissot brings out the Rock Watch

1987
Tissot introduces the Two-Timer (a watch showing both analog and digital display)

INDEX

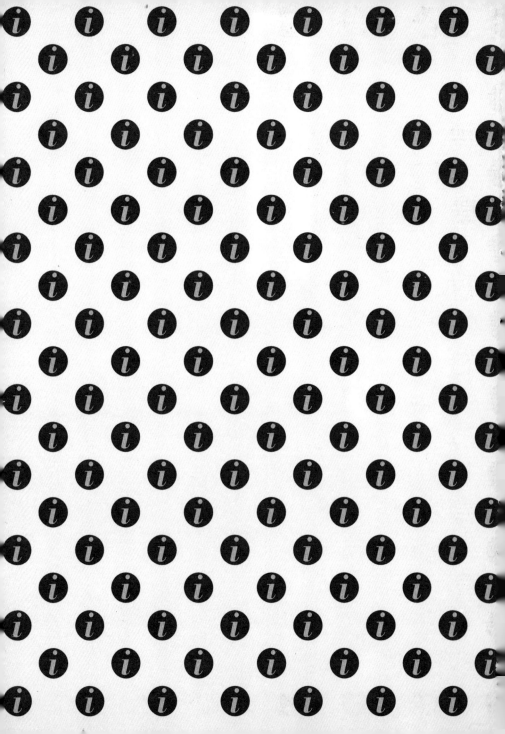